LIBRARY OF CONGRESS CATALOGING-IN-PUBLICATION DATA

BOYZ II MEN : US II YOU / MICHAEL MCCARY, NATHAN MORRIS, WANYA MORRIS & SHAWN STOCKMAN ; PRODUCED
AND EDITED BY DAVID COHEN ; PRINCIPAL PHOTOGRAPHY BY NICHOLAS KELSH ; INTRODUCTION AND INTER-
VIEWS BY DAVID SHEFF.
    P. CM.
    ISBN 0-00-225073-X (HC.) -- ISBN 0-00-649248-7 (PBK.)
    1. BOYZ II MEN (MUSICAL GROUP) 2. ROCK MUSICIANS--UNITED STATES-BIOGRAPHY.   I. MCCARY, MICHAEL.
ML421.B69B7 1995
782.42164'3'0922--DC20   95-38705
[B]   MN R95

PRINTED IN THE UNITED STATES OF AMERICA
BY R.R. DONNELLEY & SONS COMPANY

10 9 8 7 6 5 4 3 2 1

BOYZ II MEN

[US II YOU]

SHAWN

PRODUCED AND EDITED
BY DAVID COHEN

PRINCIPAL PHOTOGRAPHY
BY NICHOLAS KELSH

INTRODUCTION AND INTERVIEWS
BY DAVID SHEFF

MICHAEL

WANYA

By Michael McCary

Nathan Morris

Wanya Morris

& Shawn Stockman

CollinsPublishersSanFrancisco
A Division of HarperCollinsPublishers

Winterland productions ©1995 WINTERLAND PRODUCTIONS

NATHAN

Now and then, a pop phenomenon comes along that bucks trends. At a time when harsh, abrasive music is dominating the charts and headlines—music with violent and misogynistic lyrics that are shouted, not sung—Boyz II Men is an anachronism. Here are four young men who sing love songs with ethereal harmonies and deeply felt passion.

The music is an antidote that has been embraced by millions of people throughout the world since the group's 1991 debut album, *Cooleyhighharmony*, which sold a remarkable eight million copies. The following year, the single "End of the Road," from the soundtrack of the movie *Boomerang*, hit No. 1 on *Billboard's* charts and stayed there for thirteen weeks, breaking the record set by "Don't Be Cruel" backed with "Hound Dog" by Elvis Presley. The group beat its own record when "I'll Make Love to You," from their second LP, stayed at No. 1 for 14 weeks. It was finally knocked out of the top slot by another Boyz II Men song, "On Bended Knee." Only Presley and the Beatles had previously accomplished that feat. This time, the Boyz II Men album that contained those songs, titled, simply, *II*, went platinum 10 times—that is, it sold 10 million copies. Their Christmas album, *Christmas Interpretations*, written and produced with Brian McKnight, went double platinum. And along the way, the Boyz won dozens of awards and sold out hundreds of concerts. Their fans came to include Michael Jackson, LL Cool J, Prince, Whitney Houston, Annie Lennox, and Patti LaBelle. Even the First Family—the President of the United States, First Lady, and First Daughter, Chelsea—are Boyz II Men fans and have invited the group to the White House on several occasions.

With vocal wizardry, sizzling R&B, color-coordinated ensembles and white-hot choreography, Boyz II Men has been compared to Motown acts from decades ago—the Temptations, the Four Tops. The content of their songs—that is, love in its many incarnations, from courtship to sex to marriage and commitment—harken back to the label's superstars, including Marvin Gaye and the Supremes. But this isn't just the Motown sound updated for the 90s. Boyz II Men is breaking new ground with state-of-the-art production and beats that draw on every musical style. The results are electrifying. As a reviewer of a live performance described it, "They soundly belted out the kinds of songs that made members of the audience—male, female, black, white, old, young—throw their hands in the air and sing along at the top of their lungs." Whether they are singing "Thank You," with its thrilling, complex, super-charged rhythm and seamlessly woven vocal harmonies, or the soul-drenched *a cappella* cover of the Beatles' "Yesterday," Boyz II Men has reintroduced fantasy, love and romance, all set to an infectious beat. *Time* magazine noted, "The vocal quartet...is living, singing proof that the love song—like love itself—will never really disappear."

Boyz II Men is comprised of four immensely talented young men—Wanya Morris, Nathan Morris (no relation), Shawn Stockman, and Michael McCary—all in their early twenties, who hail from urban neighborhoods in and around Philadelphia. All raised by their mothers, with the intermittent involvement of their fathers and stepfathers, each of the Boyz was influenced by church at a time when many of their peers were spending time in and out of jail, in gangs, and dealing and using drugs. Wanya Morris recalls, "As boys, we looked out the window, saw people get blasted, people get beat up, heard about your boys getting shot up, and saw all kinds of crazy stuff happening. Even now I hear about some of my boys, boys we'd play football with or something, getting killed. To survive in that community is a rare thing." Each of the group members credits his family and God with the fact that he survived at all.

Music defined their lives and brought them together. They listened to music on the radio, on TV, and in church. They sang before they were old enough to talk, though none of them seriously imagined a career in music. Shawn Stockman was typical: "My mother listened to old Teddy Pendergrass albums, LTD, Ohio Players, Michael Jackson, Stevie Wonder," he remembers. "She loved Barry White. Loves him to this day. I sang all the time. I had a little Fisher-Price tape player and microphone. My favorite commercial would come on TV, and I would sing along and record my voice. My voice was really high back then. I played it back and was fascinated. My mother must have told everybody how I sang because I would go to the old neighborhood barbershop and the barbers would come over and ask me to sing. I didn't want to—I was afraid to sing in front of all those people. But the man in charge of the shop said, 'I'll give you five dollars.' Five dollars! That was a lot of money. Shoot! All right! So I did it. I would stand there and sing 'The Lady in My Life' by Michael Jackson or another song and get five dollars each time."

Clearly gifted, they all found their way to one of Philadelphia's treasures, the High School of Creative and Performing Arts. "A boy down the street went to the school," Michael McCary says. "It never dawned on me that I could go. But I watched the TV show *Fame* all the time. I wondered how it would be. I wondered if I would have a chance. I heard that I could audition, so when I was twelve, I went down. I sang two church tunes. And I couldn't believe it—I got in."

They all wound up in the school's choir, and when they sang together for the first time, it was sublime. Nathan Morris was one of the group's organizers and arrangers. "When we put them all together in a group, we weren't looking at personalities," he says. "We were just listening to how it sounded, and it sounded so good when we sang together. We all had basically the same musical influences and the same musical ideas. It just gelled. It took a while for the personalities to gel. We were a group before we were friends, but the music just clicked automatically. I can never explain it, but it just was something magical that happened." Michael recalls, "From the first time we sang together, there was something happening. We sang at a party at school, and afterwards, we were treated differently—as if it was the first time the whole school had seen us. It was like, 'What just happened?'"

Wanya accurately sums up the contributions of each singer: "We are different personalities and different kinds of singers. Nathan's a very strong singer. He sings baritone and high soprano with a beautiful falsetto. He's a very versatile singer; he sings everything. Michael is the foundation, the bass, the deep-voiced guy, the one who gives us that round sound. Shawn is so sweet-voiced, it's unbelievable. His voice is silky smooth. He gives people a punch in the heart. He gets me a lot because he sings so beautifully, like a butterfly. A butterfly flutters. It flies all over the place. Shawn sings like that. Me? I bring strength—hard and powerful singing—to the table. I like to be the Martin Luther

King of singing. Dr. King spoke to the masses. He touched a lot of people. That's what I try to do with my vocals. I try to be like a preacher, no matter what I'm singing about." As a *New York Times* reviewer later put it, "They sounded like a harmonically sophisticated gospel quartet or a doo-wop group.... They showed passion."

In 1989, the super-hot group Bell Biv DeVoe, comprised of former members of New Edition, were performing in Philadelphia when Boyz II Men decided, on a lark, to sneak backstage. "Biv"—Michael Bivins, one of the group members, agreed to listen to them sing. He was bowled over, immediately agreeing to represent them. It took nearly 18 months before a record deal was struck with Motown. It was a fitting marriage, since Boyz II Men carried on the tradition of the label's most famous acts. Michael McCary says he still wasn't counting on anything and took his mother's advice: "Don't base your life on a chance you might be an entertainer. It's a one-in-a-million shot, like winning the lottery. Have your education to fall back on." Michael stayed in school, studying accounting and prelaw.

With the release of *Cooleyhighharmony* in 1992, Michael had to leave accounting behind. The album contained songs the Boyz wrote themselves and ones they gathered from some hot young writer-producers—including Dallas Austin, who went on to work with Madonna. The success of this debut album was unprecedented. The second album was even more successful, and the Boyz are now the best-selling vocal group in the world.

Though their success is phenomenal, a reminder that the American dream can still come true, even in America's inner cities, the Boyz have not forgotten their roots: religion and family. They are all involved as Big Brothers, play charity basketball, and have won the NAACP Image Award. They still live in the Philadelphia area, albeit in nicer neighborhoods and fancier homes, near their extended families—parents, uncles, aunts, nieces, nephews, close friends and quite a few dogs. In a business characterized by egos and excess, they remain humble. Before and after each performance, the Boyz gather in a circle for prayer. At a recent concert, Shawn said, "Thank you, Father, for getting us here safely." It is at times like those when you get the sense that the Boyz know how far they have traveled from the projects to stardom and just how blessed they are.

Ladies and gentlemen, it gives us great pleasure to introduce: Wanya Morris...Nathan Morris...Shawn Stockman...and Michael McCary — Boyz II Men.

Wanya: We are all from urban neighborhoods in Philly. These were loving communities that turned a corner during our lifetimes. As we grew up, the neighborhoods got worse. Bad things were all around us. Gangs and drugs were on the rise. Drugs were as available as a pack of cigarettes. I sat there and I watched a lot of things happening. I saw my boys die. A lot of them.

Michael: My mom always worked, but in between jobs, she made sure we were taken care of. Even though we didn't have much, we were always all right. There was food, a roof over our heads and lots of love. There were drugs and violence outside—people on the corner selling drugs. People slinging dice. But that didn't mean you had to get involved. The difference was our upbringing. The need for attention is what makes people do bad things. They want quick money, flash. While they were out there doing that, we were studying our books. Mom taught us that the way to get all the things that you want in life is through books, not slinging any dice.

Nathan: I'm from a family of two sisters and one brother. I was the youngest. When I was about nine or ten, my mom and dad were going through a divorce. Things weren't all that great. We didn't have everything we wanted to have. There were times when there was no electricity and no gas or water. But my mom tried to make the situation better. We moved in with my grandmother for a while until my mom found something better. After that we moved to South Philly. Now that we have a better life — an easier life — I remember all we went through. It was tough on both of my parents, and they never gave up trying, trying to take care of their family. It makes me remember what it is I'm here to do. Things may be easier now, but the values don't change. I always remember where I'm from. We all do. There is no pretending to be something special, something high and mighty, when you know your roots.

Shawn: I'm from a typical black neighborhood that you'll find in southwest Philly. I lived with my mother and three brothers and sister. Everybody knew each other. Everybody looked out for each other. Yes, there were things out there to trip you up. But you didn't have to do those things. No matter what was going on outside, we were taught to pay attention to higher things. My mother taught me to read and write and to read the Bible. She instilled in me the sense of what is right and what is wrong. It lasted in me enough so that I was able to avoid trouble. If I didn't feel comfortable doing something, if it didn't feel right next to what my mother taught me, I wouldn't do it.

Wanya: Drugs got the best of my mother, just like my boys who I was hanging around with. It got the best of them. Money was coming in, but it wasn't enough because now she was doing drugs. She was doing it for us, selling drugs to get money, but we would have preferred having no money. You can't help a person doing drugs. It made our life hard, very hard. Worse came to worse. I wasn't scared because everybody knew me, and I never did anything bad to anybody, but I was growing up fast because there was nobody else to raise us. I was still young, didn't know what was going on, but you do what you have to do. A lot of things happened during the years my mom was on drugs and was trying to get off. For a time, we were on welfare. Welfare was cool. I was still Wanya. I learned to look at everything carefully, to analyze everything. I was raised by everybody living in the projects. That's what grew me up. Growing up in the projects made me grow older more quickly than anybody.

BACKSTAGE

TOP AND CENTER: SHAWN AND WANYA LOOSEN UP BACKSTAGE AT THE
SONY/BLOCKBUSTER ARENA. BOTTOM: NATHAN AND MICHAEL ENJOY A RARE QUIET MOMENT
BEFORE GOING ON STAGE. THE BOXES OF FLOWERS ARE FOR THE BOYZ' MOTHERS
WHO ATTENDED THE HOMETOWN PHILADELPHIA-AREA SHOW.

Michael: I listened to music all my life. My mom always played music. There was always music going on. My brother would have the radio on all day long. I loved the Temptations. I would see them on the TV. To me it wasn't old music; I never knew how long they had been around. All I knew was that it was good music. I listened to New Edition and everything else on the radio. I was always singing, singing along with whatever I heard. Even when I was going down the street, I was humming. I didn't take notice about being an entertainer until I was twelve and got into the High School of Creative and Performing Arts. A whole world opened up there—everyone there was passionate about music the way I was, whether it was classical music or jazz, popular music or the gospel we sang in the choir.

Nathan: We were all in the same choir at school. That's how we met, though we didn't know each other at first. Now we're like a family. When we're on the road, we are together more than we are with our real families—but it wasn't like that at first.

Shawn: I kept to myself. I was a nerd, spending all my time reading comics and listening to metal music. I definitely was not in the hip crowd like the others. The others were more social. I didn't really get to know them until later. Nathan was hanging around the cool kids—the popular student body kids and all the good singers. He was the suave guy who dated all the girls in the choir. Wanya came into the choir later. When he did, he hung around with Nathan. Definitely cool, too. I hung around with the least popular kids in the school. I was always quiet, always on my own. I don't think I could go back to any of my elementary and junior high schools and see anyone who would remember me. I've thought about going back, but it wouldn't make any difference because no one would know me. Well, maybe they would know me now.

Nathan: We were sort of organizing a singing group, using different members of the choir. Finally we had Shawn, Wanya, a friend named Marc Nelson and myself together, singing as a group. We hadn't met Michael yet. One day, the four of us were singing in the bathroom, practicing in there. The song was "Can You Stand the Rain?" by New Edition. Michael happened to come in and, without anyone saying a word, he started singing, adding the bass note. It was what we needed, tied the whole thing together. We were calling ourselves Unique Attraction, but we didn't think it fit us so Shawn and I were trying to think up a new name. At the time, we were listening to the radio when New Edition's "Boys to Men" came on. That's where we got it.

Shawn: The first time we sang in public was in the winter of 1988 at a club in Philadelphia called The Impulse. We sang three songs: "Can You Stand the Rain?," "A Thousand Miles Away," and "What's Your Name?" The reaction was *whoosh*. Something good was definitely going on. We had tough times when we were starting out. We weren't best friends yet. We had to work on respecting each other, understanding where each one came from. But from the start we had this common ground: the music. The more we sang together, the more we blended.

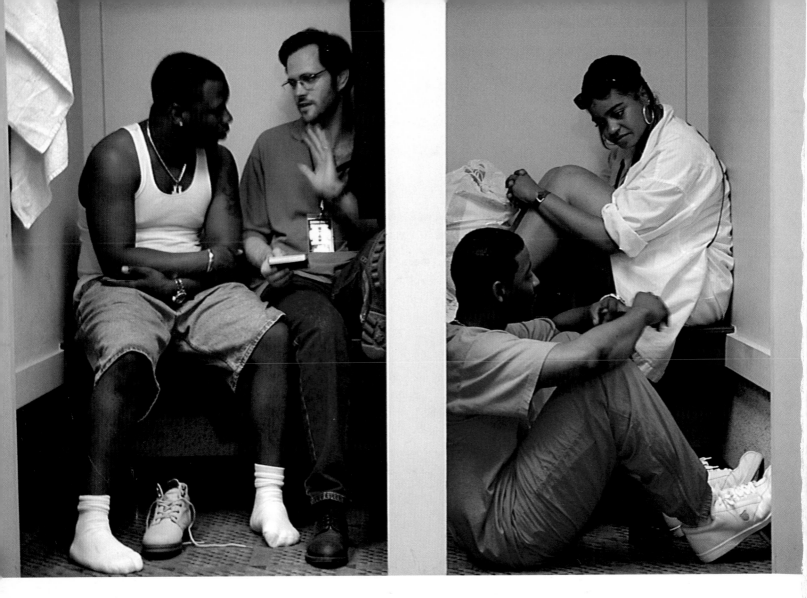

IN THE DRESSING ROOMS OF RFK STADIUM IN WASHINGTON DC WANYA GETS DOWN TO BUSINESS WITH BOYZ II MEN CO-MANAGER JOHN DUKAKIS WHILE MICHAEL CHATS WITH A FAN.

Michael: It was just for fun up until the point we snuck backstage at a Bell Biv DeVoe concert and found Michael Bivins. We asked if we could sing for him and—well, we just sang. He said, "There is a possibility that you guys can do this." We were still skeptical, but he said he was going to get us a record deal. Eventually, he got us signed up to Motown. He made it a reality. I stayed in school—I wasn't assuming we would make it. Before we made the record, we did a bunch of backgrounds for other people, like Stevie Wonder. Then the record came out, and we were opening for MC Hammer's tour. During a break, we recorded "End of the Road," a song Babyface, L A Reid and Daryl Simmons wrote for the soundtrack of *Boomerang*. What can you say about it? It came out and was one of the biggest selling singles of all time. That launched things into a whole new level. It was a straightforward line from there. The question then was, "What do you do next? How can you measure up and stay fresh?" That was the challenge.

Wanya: We work hard to come up with new ideas, new, intricate harmonies, pretty harmonies, harmonies that go off into different directions. We just try things out. Any one of us might start singing, and soon we are all into the song, seeing where it goes. We sing every type of music, but we all like the idea of singing songs that take us—and can take the audience—away from everyday life. We could get into a lot of other things, like political rap, talking about what's going on in the world. But that's not what we're interested in. You can look at the news if you want to be aware of what's going on in the world. We want to give people something else to grab hold of. We want to make music to ease your mind. We want to give people love songs, to make them feel good, to make them forget their troubles, to make them feel love. More than any other type of music, slow songs are what inspire me. A fast song is all right, but a slow song can get inside you. You know the feeling when the slow songs come on. You are down in the basement with your girlfriend. The music comes on and—mmm. You get to hold your woman. You get to feel love. There isn't anything better.

GEAR FOR THE YEAR-LONG "ALL AROUND THE WORLD" TOUR INCLUDES A CUSTOM-MADE CASE TO CARRY THE GROUP'S 40 PAIRS OF SHOES.

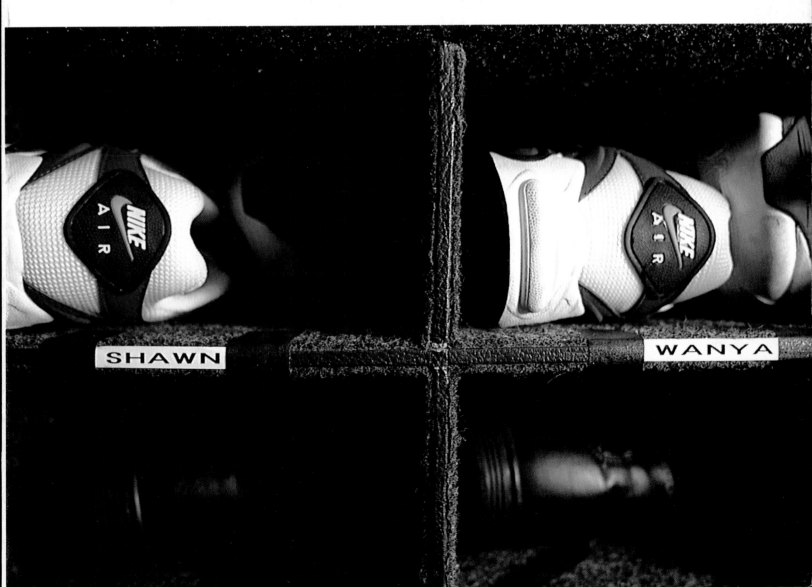

THESE PAGES: AN HOUR BEFORE SHOWTIME IN HOMETOWN PHILLY.

FOLLOWING PAGES: SHAWN AND NATHAN SIT IN ON A SOUND CHECK WITH THE BAND IN BOSTON.

MEET AND GREET: (CLOCKWISE FROM TOP RIGHT) NATHAN SHAKES HANDS
WITH WASHINGTON MAYOR MARION BARRY WHILE WANYA VISITS WITH SINGER PATTI LABELLE,
NEW YORK KNICKS STAR PATRICK EWING, AND MEMBERS OF THE WENCH MOB
—A DANCE ENSEMBLE THAT PERFORMS WITH SINGERS TLC. NATHAN AND MAYOR BARRY ARE
ACCOMPANIED BY SUZANNE EL-AMIN, THE WIFE OF BOYZ II MEN CO-MANAGER QADREE EL-AMIN.

MICHAEL BENCH-PRESSES 140 POUNDS UNDER THE WATCHFUL EYE OF TRAINER "BIG MIKE"; HAIR STYLIST CRAIG DOGGETT TOUCHES UP SHAWN, AND WANYA PUMPS-UP BEFORE THE SHOW IN BOSTON.

Michael: It doesn't matter where we are—at home, touring, at concert halls. We pray a lot. We're always praying.

Nathan: With the spiritual background that my family has bestowed on me, I have somewhere else to go, something to lean on, and someone to believe in who is always there. I pray, and it reminds me of the basics.

Wanya: I go by a lot of the ways of the Lord. I'm not perfect at all, but I know that I give the Lord glory for everything that I do. When things were going wrong in my life, I would visit with my mom. She told me, "I want you to read right here," and she would point to the Scripture. Then all the worries would be gone. Now I pray, and it eases the mind. It can be my inspiration. It's like a cleansing.

SHOWTIME

FIRE AND RAIN: FANS IN SPRINGFIELD MA ROAR AS AN EXPLOSION OF FLAMES PUNCTUATES THE GROUP'S FIRST NUMBER. NATHAN SINGS THE TOP-10 SINGLE "WATER RUNS DRY" DURING A SIMULATED ON-STAGE RAINSTORM.

Nathan: When we are performing, we feel what the audience is feeling. We put everything into it to try to make them feel like they were part of the song — part of the song when it was created and part of the emotion behind singing it. As performers, if the crowd is not into it, your job is to go out and get them. You try to do it with looks and expressions, with whatever it takes. You can make an individual feel special. Then you can look to the back of the hall, way back, and try to get everyone there. It can start to feel like a job, but usually something happens in the course of a night. It depends on how you feel before you go on. You may be tired; you may have had a bad day; you may be thinking about everything except what you need to be thinking about. But then when the lights come on and the music begins, you're taken over. The crowd is energized. The crowd is wild. The lights are blazing, and there is this roar.

Wanya: There are a lot of fans out there who really love us. God bless them. It's something: These four brothers from Philadelphia are known all over the world.

Shawn: You see a girl in the audience who is breaking down in tears. That's what you perform for. That's what you go on stage every night to see.

Wanya: We vibe off the audience. A lot of times you want to touch that person who isn't being touched—or the person with the attitude that they can't be touched. I can close my eyes on the stage and be whatever I want to be. I can actually close my eyes and picture the whole place empty. Then, when I open my eyes, it is empty. Or I can only see the people I want to see and hear the people I want to hear. If I want to, I can see only one person. I can look at that person and be a preacher and make the people feel what I'm saying. If I want, I can close my eyes and say, "Today you're going to sing your ass off," and I do it. Or I can close my eyes and say, "I'm the sexiest man in the world: Be sexy," and then I go on the stage and grab 'em.

ABOVE: NATHAN SINGS "YOUR LOVE" TO A LUCKY LADY IN CAMDEN NJ.
LEFT: MICHAEL CROONS "ON BENDED KNEE" IN SPRINGFIELD MA.

Nathan: I sang because I loved singing. It was a part of my life and a part of who I was. I never wanted to grow up to be a superstar, never even thought about it. The first time I thought about making a living as a singer was when we got our record deal. It just sneaked up on me. I guess that's the kind of person that I am.

Michael: When everybody's just moving and screaming, your adrenaline just pumps so high that you are going a million steps a minute. You're still focused on what you're doing, but you're just so happy, you're so ecstatic that everybody's enjoying what you're doing. You keep going and push and push and push until you have nothing else to give.

WANYA IN THE SPOTLIGHT.

FOLLOWING PAGES: EACH SINGER'S MIKE RESTS ON THE SOUNDBOARD BEFORE THE BOSTON
CONCERT. WANYA'S IS YELLOW; SHAWN'S, BLUE; NATHAN'S, RED; AND MICHAEL'S, GREEN.

WANYA:

WHO WROTE THE BOOK OF

LOVE?

GOD WROTE THE BOOK

OF LOVE.

SHAWN WANYA MIKE   NATE   AUD   PCM 70   PCM

TAR   EAR MIX   EAR MIX   MIC   L.   R.   L.

ACC.

BOYZ II MEN PERFORMED IN MORE THAN 70 CITIES ACROSS AMERICA DURING
THE 1994-95 "ALL AROUND THE WORLD" TOUR.

FOLLOWING PAGES: FIFTY CANDLES BURN BRIGHT AND ALL IS RIGHT...
AS THE AUDIENCE LIGHTS UP FOR WANYA.

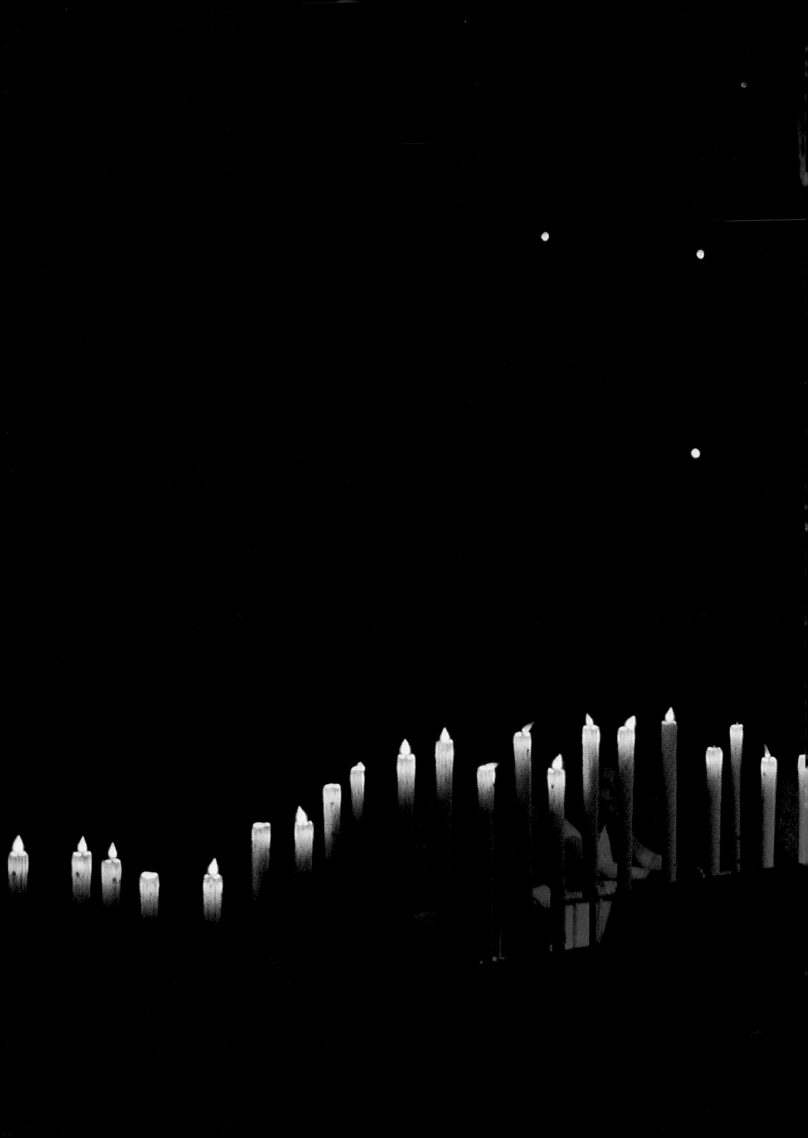

ABOVE: IN 95° HEAT, MASSACHUSETTS FANS WERE HOSED OFF, CARTED
OFF STAGE AND THEN AWESTRUCK DURING THE SHOW.

RIGHT: THE FIREWORKS FLY DURING THE SHOW STOPPER, "MOTOWNPHILLY."

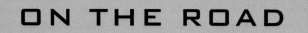

ON THE ROAD

ABOVE AND RIGHT: IN A MINIVAN IN SPRINGFIELD MA AND ON THE BUS IN WASHINGTON DC.

Nathan: We keep it sane and fun on the road as much as we can. Playing sports, playing video games, writing music, shopping. We try to get away from the work.

Shawn: Sometimes it feels as if we live together on the bus, traveling from city to city, driving all night long. We could be arguing really deep about girls or whatever and we start to laugh like it's the most ridiculous thing. It's like in a family.

Michael: We know each other so well that we can push exactly the right button if we want to do some teasing. But it's all in fun. We're never trying to pierce someone's heart. But if your socks don't match, watch out.

Wanya: We help each other keep it in perspective. We are each other's level heads. We check each other. "Yo, man, that's not cool." And we listen. It's exactly like a family unit. We keep together—open with each other, trusting each other. That way nobody can break us apart.

PREVIOUS PAGES: AN MTV CREW IN BOSTON CATCHES MICHAEL COMING OFF ONE OF THE FOUR BUSES THAT TRANSPORT THE GROUP, BAND, MANAGEMENT, AND CREW FROM CITY TO CITY.

Michael: It's definitely like a family. Every single day it's Shawn, Nate, Mike, and Wanya together on the road.

Shawn: We take turns with our moods. Sometimes I am the solemn one, sometimes Nathan, sometimes Wanya, sometimes Michael. The bus is our home away from home. It's where we can be laughing, acting stupid. We can be ourselves.

Wanya: Shawn is ultimately a nice guy. He wants problems not to exist. He thinks of ways to make things right. He vibes off everything. He doesn't say much until something bothers him. Mike keeps to himself, plays basketball a lot. He sees the beauty in a lot of situations that no one else does. He's hard to get to know. He knows a lot about money. Mike is going to be rich. He's a prankster. We call him "devil boy." He's definitely the foundation. Nate believes a lot in this organization. He wants it to be sparkling clean. He believes so much in family life. He's an unbelievably nice guy. I don't know what I would have done without them. I just can't say. God helped me find them.

ABOVE: MICHAEL ENJOYS ONE OF WANYA'S JOKES.
LEFT: AFTER THE RFK STADIUM GIG, MICHAEL SETTLES INTO HIS BUNK FOR THE LONG NIGHT-DRIVE
TO BOSTON. THE GROUP FLIES ONLY IF THE ROAD TRIP WOULD BE LONGER THAN 12 HOURS.

Michael: The bus, going to the next city, is sleep time. We may do a lot of goofing off, playing video games, hanging, playing music, working on new songs, cracking jokes. We love to laugh. We laugh all day long—but then it's time to crawl into your bunk and say, "All right. Let me regroup."

We're all together on the bus. We're with these folks more than with our actual family. You know what I'm saying? It's like every single day, you're with these four together, whereas with your family, you may see them once a month, if that. We are together every waking minute—when we're going to sleep, when we're on stage, when we're in meetings or doing interviews—all day long. Quite naturally, we're more than just friends. Quite naturally, like brothers, just like any other household, we get into arguments about the silliest things, but it's just like a regular family now, a close-knit family.

Nathan: We're always on the move and there's not a lot of time to think. When I do reflect on my life, I think back on the people of my neighborhood—this rugged, hard, urban neighborhood. I think how fortunate we all are to have gotten out. Many people don't. There were all these problems, all these temptations. We didn't have the traditional American family to help us, not after my mother and father divorced. My mother was always there, encouraging me, and my father did what he could—though he wasn't around after a point. I see him all the time now, but not then. I don't hold nothing against him for that. I guess relationships go the way they go. I don't know what happened—they had their personal differences, and I can't fault him. One thing I know: You only get one father, and you must cherish him.

A THOUGHTFUL NATHAN ON THE BUS IN WASHINGTON DC.

SHAWN ENJOYS ROOM SERVICE AND A BALL GAME IN SPRINGFIELD. THE LARGE CASE CONTAINS HIS RECORDING AND MIXING EQUIPMENT.

Shawn: I never think I'm the sexiest guy in the world. No matter how many girls are out there screaming their heads off. When I'm alone in my hotel room, it's not hard to put it in perspective. It's the music that affects them. The songs are what people fall in love with. At its best, it's like catching the spirit in church. When you see one person feeling the holy spirit all up in them, it excites you. Then it spreads. It comes from somewhere else. You can't help but be taken over, too. After a while the whole church is up and dancing and shouting. So it's not me up there. I know I'm not the handsomest guy in the world. And it's not only this sex thing that girls respond to. We are very respectful of the women in our lives. We appreciate what women go through. We feel that the man should be the one to be supportive of the woman, to be there for her at the end of the day.

SHAWN GROOMS FOR THE SPRINGFIELD SHOW.

Shawn: When we were growing up, we saw guys that could afford it with their gold chains and big cables around their necks, with huge bracelets and gold rings on every finger. It looked appealing from where we sat, watching them walk down the street, looking all cool and fly. It was something that we never had and always wanted. I would walk home from school and go by the jewelry place and stare at the stuff in the windows and think about what I would buy. It was pretty silly—I'm glad now that I couldn't afford that stuff. It was pretty gaudy, you know? But it meant something to us as kids. It meant success that we did not have. Also, we saw rappers on TV. They had their big Mercedes Benzes and nice clothes and sparkling, shiny jewelry, girls hanging on them, and they were walking down the street looking hip, and we definitely wanted to be like that. A lot of the guys we saw on the street were trying to look like the ones on TV. But one thing I noticed when I was a kid was that they were all neat—with nice shirts, pressed jeans, clean white sneakers, and a fresh haircut. My mother taught us to be neat and clean even if we didn't have expensive clothes. She never allowed us to go outside looking like a bum, looking disorderly. She always combed our hair, made sure our sneakers were clean and there were no holes in our shirts before we could go out, even if we were just going out to play. That's still with me. It's not about being boastful or showing off. It's pride in yourself. That's what it was to her.

The others in the group tease me about how neat I am all the time. I'll think I'm looking slovenly, wearing sweat pants that are rolled up and some sneakers and a T-shirt and they are ragging on me for being neat. Actually we're all like that in a way. It's part of the Boyz II Men look. We all like to wear nice things. We all like to look good, though there are days when we let it all slide. At home I don't get a haircut, let my beard grow real thick, wear a hat down over my face and really baggy jeans and some boots and I hop in the car, no jewelry or anything. Maybe only my Rolex watch. But even then, even in certain situations where it doesn't matter how you look, I am never slummish to the point of being offensive or nasty looking. I still have neatness to it. It's just been ingrained in me.

WANYA CURLS 80 LBS. OF IRON WHILE
HIS SISTER DOROTHY THORNTON LOOKS
ON. THEN DOROTHY GIVES IT A TRY.

Wanya: We spend so much time away from home. You do what you can to keep sane. It's fun. We have a good time. But it can get to you. You work out to keep your body in shape and read for your mind. When there's time, we do our own things, working on music, going to the mall. We see each other almost every day, but it's still fun, though the most fun is being on stage.

I went out to a mall the other day and was seeing how the gangster rap lifestyle is changing people's lives, even for people who are not in these gangs. Folks think, "Look at these brothers, dang, these brothers are cool." I mean, *I* even look at them: Hey, man, that brother's mellow, you know what I mean, with the sandals, the socks pulled up to his calves, and the shorts, just walking around? It's all influential. Well, *we* want to influence people some other way — not glorifying gangs, but glorifying love and family. When I saw that, I was thinking that I feel like a leader, and I'm proud to be a leader with something else to say. Maybe some brothers are listening.

Sometimes in the audience there might be a girl out there who is with a brother, and he's sitting there like this with his arms folded and his girl is right next to him, like, "God, I can't get too excited; I can't scream. He'll be mad at me." You just focus on that girl, at least make her smile. You get that smile and you're happy. It ain't about trying to get my man's girl. It's about that challenge, you know?

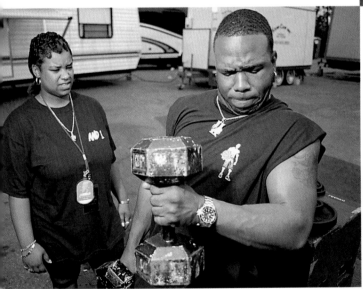

Sometimes I'll bring my boys — friends from the neighborhood — out on the road to let them see what's going on. Or I bring my brother and sisters to let them see. For us it's the usual thing, but for them it's still exciting. My little sister has come out. And my sister Dorothy sometimes works with us on the road. To have the family around is a blessing. It's so good to be able to share with them.

IN THE STUDIO

Shawn: I can't lie—I've been enjoying myself for these last four years. I've done basically everything that I've dreamt of doing and then some. Met people I never thought I'd ever meet. Accomplished a lot. You are singing and doing what you love to do—doing what you would do for fun, for no money—and you look up and there you see some of the greatest singers and musicians in the world. It keeps you humble, because you want to be worthy of singing with them. And it keeps you working hard, because you want it to be as great as you can be.

Wanya: It's unbelievable to work with the people we have worked with. I can't begin to say how it feels. We have met people we grew up listening to. People we looked at. Looked up to. God, I wanted to be like them.

Michael: It really took us by surprise to have so many entertainers as fans now. Someone will come back stage and say, "Prince is in the audience," or we'll hear that Michael Jackson likes our music and wants to work with us. Now we're recording in our own studio with LL Cool, who is one of our heroes. We've heard so many nice things—from the biggest stars in the world. Every now and then it hits us, like, "Wow! What are we doing?" But you can't really harp on your accomplishments, because there's always too much to do.

PREVIOUS PAGES AND ABOVE: RAPPER LL COOL J ARRIVES AT THE BOYZ' OWN STONECREEK STUDIO
OUTSIDE PHILADELPHIA TO RECORD THE SONG, "HEY LOVER" FOR HIS UPCOMING ALBUM.
EACH OF THE BOYZ LAID HIS VOCALS DOWN, THEN LL COOL J RAPPED HIS PART IN ONE TAKE.

PRIVATE TIME WITH
SHAWN

SHAWN ARRIVES HOME ON A RARE DAY OFF FROM THE "ALL AROUND THE WORLD" TOUR. HE RECEIVES A BIG HUG FROM HIS MOM, JOANNE STOCKMAN.

I know I've come a long way from the home I grew up in, though I still feel as if I'm a part of it. Along with the hard work in this business comes the spoils. It's not hard for me to keep it in perspective. My goal was to live nicely. If I hadn't done it this way, I would have tried to do it some other way. I like living with beautiful things around, having nice clothes, a nice house. I like being able to hop into a really nice car and not having to worry about it breaking down. But it doesn't mean everything to me. I definitely don't forget where I got it all and that keeps my head in perspective. The things around me don't rule me. It's great to have nice things—I'm not going to lie. But they don't rule me. I work hard, but the ultimate place it comes from is not from me but from the Lord. The success we have had was part of my vision and the Lord blessed me to see it through. I never forget that.

CLOCKWISE FROM UPPER LEFT: ON HIS DAY OFF, SHAWN TRIES OUT A NEW TUNE ON HIS KEYBOARD, PLAYS BASKETBALL AT A NEIGHBOR'S HOUSE, MODELS HIS "MICHAEL JACKSON WANNABE HAT," AND SPENDS TIME IN HIS HOME OFFICE.

My mom gave me a different perspective on life—a perspective that I need at times. She's into simple things. Things you get from loving and struggling. It helps me to remember that. She believes in the Lord. What the Lord says goes. She keeps everything clear and simple, even when the fears come in. Sometimes I get afraid of what is happening to me, of what might happen to me, and she helps me to remember the Lord. She says that it is the Lord who is the one that's blessing you with all this— with the people around you as well as all the things that come with success. If you give Him his just due, if you keep Him close to your heart, then everything will be all right. Even if I went broke, even if I went to the poorhouse, even if I went back to 39th and Belmount, the neighborhood where I grew up, as long as the Lord is with me, I'll have peace of mind and the vision to accept what I have.

SHAWN SAYS GRACE WITH HIS MOM BEFORE LUNCH AT THEIR FAVORITE ITALIAN RESTAURANT.

SHAWN WATCHES AN ANNOUNCEMENT FOR THE MTV VIDEO AWARDS. BOYZ II MEN WERE NOMINATED FOR THEIR "WATER RUNS DRY" VIDEO.

FOLLOWING PAGES: A QUIET MOMENT ON THE BANKS OF A STREAM NEAR SHAWN'S HOUSE.

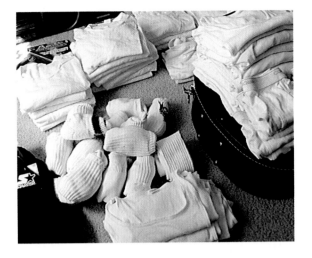

SHAWN'S MOM WASHED AND FOLDED HIS UNDERWEAR AND SOCKS FOR THE NEXT LEG OF THE TOUR.

Sometimes I think too much has happened to us too fast. It's hard to really catch up with it, hard to grasp it. I was sitting in my room listening to some music thinking about how time moves. It's all going so fast that it's hard to really enjoy all the amazing things going on in my life now. Things are moving too fast to enjoy the simple things, like a kiss from a girl that loves you. I'm not able to experience that, to experience those small things that mean something to a person. I'm not able to enjoy the small things that meant something to me in the past. There are things I enjoyed so much that I can't do now. I don't have time. I can't go walking in the park or sit alone for hours. Or just walk — to walk around from neighborhood to neighborhood. I would take really long walks with my father. He would take me on long walks in the park. We would take the long route instead of the quick route through town. We would go through the trees with our walking sticks. The Lord has blessed me beyond belief, but there's a price to pay.

PRIVATE TIME WITH
NATHAN

ABOVE: NATHAN GIVES AN AUTOGRAPH TO NEIGHBOR MICHELLE STIMPSON.
RIGHT: NATHAN IS TALKING TO HIS MOTHER, GALE HARRIS, WHEN A FAN JUMPS OUT OF HER CAR FOR A HUG.

This life has its glamour, but it is very difficult. We work hard. It's demanding—very, very demanding. Our lives have changed in every way. They say your friends don't change, but they do. They say the music industry doesn't have to change you, either, but it does. It changes everyone. It may not change you for the worse, but it changes you. Your lifestyle is different. Your perception of the world is different. You don't always have the personal time that you want. Your time is scheduled from the moment you wake up until the moment you go to sleep. You're pulled in a hundred directions at any given time. A lot of artists pull their hair out because they try to figure out how to please everybody. When people approach you, they always want you to stop right away. They don't realize that this is the only free time that you may have to do what you want to do, and if you stop for everyone your time is gone. Some people understand, but some give attitude. That goes back to the saying that you can't please everybody. You can only do your best.

PREVIOUS PAGES: NATHAN READS IN HIS SANCTUARY JUST OFF HIS BEDROOM.

NATHAN:

THE FIRST MUSIC I HEARD WAS

IN CHURCH. THAT CHURCH MUSIC

FILLED MY LIFE. BESIDES

THAT, MY BIGGEST INFLUENCE WAS

SAM COOKE. I'M A SAM COOKE FAN,

ALWAYS WILL BE.

LEFT: NATHAN AT HIS KURZWEIL PIANO WITH ALEX, THE OLDEST OF HIS THREE DALMATIANS.

When my father was around, he had a spiritual influence on me that never let go. He kept us in church what seemed like 24 hours a day. Sunday, Monday, Tuesday, Wednesday, Thursday, Friday, Saturday. We didn't miss a day. I would get upset that I couldn't be outside playing with my friends, but now that I've grown up I realize and believe that he changed our lives. Even after he left, when my parents split up, those lessons stuck. And I know that if he didn't do that for us, I wouldn't be doing what I'm doing today. I wouldn't have been on the path that lead me here.

You wonder sometimes why people take drugs, why people get in gangs. Instead of letting money go to your head, you should let the Lord go to your head! I was taught that money is the root of all evil, and I understand that money is just a means of survival while you're here. It is fine to have nice things. When we were kids, we couldn't always get them. If it was gone, I'd be fine. The same things that sustain me now will always sustain me—my family and my faith. I always know where my blessings flow from. In the meantime, it feels awfully good to be able to provide for my family, to provide for my mom and dad, in a way that I never could have imagined.

RIGHT: NATHAN'S HAT, JEWELRY AND SHOE COLLECTIONS.

ABOVE: STAYING IN SHAPE KEEPS NATHAN
RELAXED BOTH ON AND OFF THE ROAD.

RIGHT: NATHAN'S OFFICE AT THE STONE-
CREEK STUDIO INCLUDES A MEMENTO OF A
MEETING WITH PRESIDENT AND MRS. CLINTON.

We've seen the president four times now.
Coming from where I did, I never really
had a fantasy about meeting the president. I never even could have imagined
it. I wasn't too much into politics.
Coming from an urban area like Philly,
you are just trying to survive in your
environment. But now opportunities like
that are coming at us all the time. You
just take it in stride. You're respectful.
You appreciate the chances that come
along. But we don't have time to think
about it much. We've always got something else to get ready for.

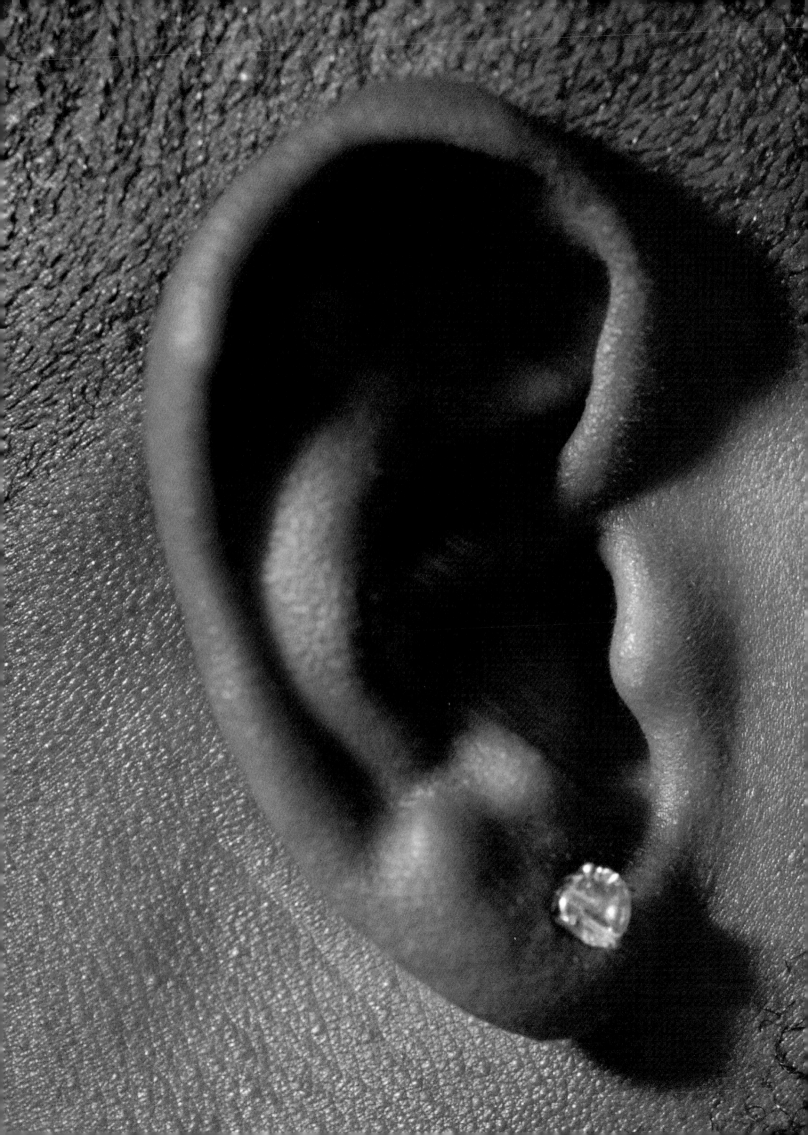

PRIVATE TIME WITH
WANYA

LEFT AND ABOVE: BOYZ II MEN SHOWS END AROUND MIDNIGHT, SO WHEN WANYA IS HOME, HE USUALLY SLEEPS UNTIL NOON. THIS MORNING HE IS AWAKENED BY A PHONE CALL.

No, my family was not the traditional family of mom and dad and a white picket fence. It wasn't that way at all. I don't know if we would have turned out to be the people that we are if it would have been that way.

I wish that people, back in the days when it was all starting—the drugs and crack—would have realized what that life was going to do to the youth as we got older. It did a job on us. It shouldn't be this way. There should be more hope. Me, I was lucky. Even when there were problems around, even when it all looked bleak because we had so little, I had the sense to keep in the good direction.

God blessed me unbelievably just keeping me alive. One thing I know: music saved me.

Music was always a very, very big part of my life. Growing up, my mom was in a singing group. They sang around the house all the time. I went to their rehearsals. My dad, when he was there, was in a singing group, too. He is one of the baddest drum players I've ever heard. I used to hang around my grandmom's where they had rehearsals in the basement. No matter which parent I was with, there was music, back and forth—always music. My grandmom listened to the radio, and it was like everywhere I went someone was singing. When I was just a small child, my grandpa and I would get in the shower together, and we would howl. He would sing, "You ain't got no drawers on," and we sang it over and over and over. All kinds of oldies, too, like "Hush Your Mouth" and "Monkey and the Buzzard."

My singing skill came from the radio, mocking what was on there, taking it all in and thinking, I can do that. Even before that, three days after they brought me home from the hospital, they tell me I was singing. My mom said that she was ironing some clothes and singing, and I would be singing the same tune back. I'd use the same notes, though I didn't say the words. She told my grandma and she didn't believe it, so my mom said, "Come down and see." Everyone said they knew I was going to be into singing. I listened to everything: the radio, Mom, Dad, everything from popular music to classical. I wanted to listen to rap but my dad, when he started coming by on weekends, wanted to feed me something else. That's where the gospel music came in.

RIGHT: WANYA TRIES TO ENJOY HIS MORNING BUBBLE BATH DESPITE THE PHOTOGRAPHER STANDING ON THE SINK.

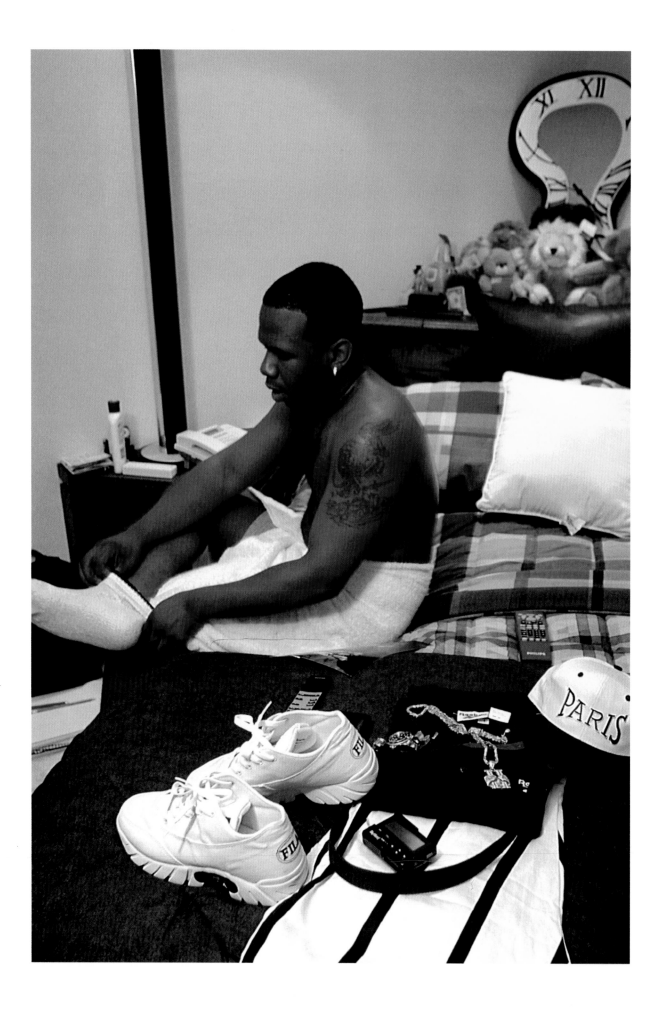

WANYA IS A FASTIDIOUS DRESSER.

Money was the case—that is, a big thing
in everybody's life back in the days when
we were kids. Clothing was becoming
important to us. The gear was becoming
higher. I didn't have the clothes. I never
stunk or nothing like that, but I didn't
have the clothes. Everybody was dressed
in Adidas and I would have Kangaroos;
or everybody had on Kangaroos, and I
had on Pro-Keds. I was always two years
late with the gig. And jobs weren't pay-
ing. That's when some brothers turned to
selling drugs. They test it, and they like
it. Some of them are still strung out.
Some are dead. Now it's fun not to be
worrying about money. I think back,
man, and it was not too long ago—four
years ago—I was living in the projects.
Four years ago I was living in the projects. I think on that.

LEFT: JACKIE THORNTON RAISED WANYA FROM THE AGE OF EIGHT. HERE JACKIE AND WANYA READ FROM PROVERBS 3:5-6 ABOUT TRUSTING THE LORD TO GUIDE YOU. THESE ARE IMPORTANT WORDS FOR BOTH JACKIE AND WANYA.

ABOVE: WANYA ALSO REMAINS CLOSE TO HIS MOTHER, CARLA MORRIS, HIS YOUNGER BROTHER, KERI, AND HIS SISTER, SERENE, WHO LIVE NEARBY.

Gospel holds a special place for me. It holds a special place for all of us. Listening to gospel music in church helped me learn how to sing on stage. You would go into church and see people sing, see how people react. I saw how music can be inspirational, how music can raise people up, lull them, inspire them. I use it all when I am singing.

My father and the woman he married came by when I was eight. They came back later and tried to help me. I would go over there, and they turned me into more of a gentleman-type person. You watch and see, and you listen. She helped teach me about God. When I was growing up, I didn't really know too much about God. I would say my prayers and go to sleep, but I didn't understand. They really brought God into my life. Jackie let me know the value of a lot of things—of life, of marriage. She made me hold the door for my sister. She taught me manners and respect. A lot of men treat women badly. They give them no respect, but she taught me to respect women.

ABOVE: WANYA WORKS OUT ON HIS BASEMENT DRUM SET. WANYA'S DAD IS A DRUMMER.

LEFT: WANYA AND HIS FATHER, DALLAS THORNTON, LOVE VIDEO FOOTBALL. WANYA USUALLY CHOOSES THE SAN FRANCISCO 49ERS AND DALLAS TAKES THE COWBOYS. THE FINAL SCORE OF THIS GAME IS DALLAS 55, WANYA 21.

Growing up, all of the pulls in the neighborhood were to go in the direction of trouble, not to get out, not to make something of yourself. It was the love of my family that kept me out of that, and the love of life itself. My family's love came strong, came with joy. They saw the sons and daughters of other families dropping. They saw those children dropping in every direction, and they didn't want to see me go that way. They wanted more for me.

PRIVATE TIME WITH
MICHAEL

I only live about 15 minutes from where I grew up, and I go down there all the time. It's a reminder that we have to do what we can for the community. I try to do my part. We play charity basketball games and raise money for Big Brothers and Big Sisters and other organizations that help. I think our success has affected us for the better. We are able now to put our families in better positions in life, to buy them homes, make sure they're comfortable. And we're in the position to help others, which feels good. We have no illusions about who we are. We're the same people we always were — the same people. Success just enhances how you were in the beginning. If you have solid values, they come along with you. We may get a lot of attention when we're on stage, but when we get off, we're just Shawn, Wanya, Nate, and Mike again. As for me, I still enjoy the same things. When I can, I want to go to the movies, to just relax, to take a walk, to sit down with my family and watch some TV, to talk and see how things have been going while we've been away. The biggest forces in my life are my mother and my brother, the same people as before. When they have something to say, I listen. They're older, and I am not a hard-headed kind of person who has to experience it for myself when people are trying to save me from some kind of embarrassment or pain.

NEAR HIS HOME IN SUBURBAN PHILADELPHIA, MICHAEL WALKS HIS DOGS, ROCKY AND CLEO, WITH HIS BROTHER, ROBERT "STRETCH" MCCARY AND ROBERT'S SON, DEMETRIUS.

It didn't matter that I'm the youngest. My mom taught me how to cook, how to do dishes, how to mop the floors, the whole nine. On trash day, we took out the trash. We cleaned and ironed and did it all, everything there was to do, learning how to get on in life.

I can get fancier food, but baked beans and hot dogs are what we love. Grew up on it and love it. Here's the recipe: open a can of beans, get some hot dogs, and cook them together.

I love animals. I love dogs. I'm comfortable when there are animals around. That's what home is to me, the place where I'm comfortable, don't have pressure to be somewhere, to do something. That's how it is with my family, my few close friends. The others in the group and I hang together at home. We meet quite often and talk about whatever is on our minds.

We need home to be a place that is tranquil, a peaceful atmosphere. We need to sit back and say: "All right, cool, let's go to the movies. Let's play pool," or whatever—or just sit there. Sit back and say, "Wow, okay, this is how it feels to relax." It's sort of pathetic. We do nothing. It's not like we're out to clubs all night. We're just home.

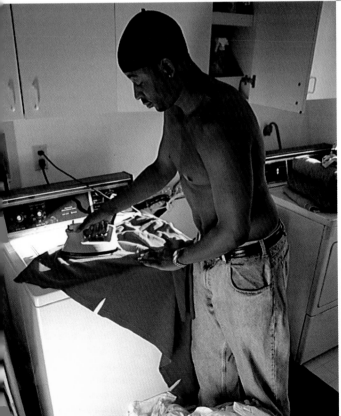

ABOVE AND RIGHT: MICHAEL AND DEMETRIUS COOL OFF ON A HOT SUMMER AFTERNOON IN PHILADELPHIA.

Taking care of my family is the thing that means the most to me—to make sure that my mom is all right, that my brother and his family are all right. Our families are the most important thing in all of our lives. Without them, we're nothing. I want my own family when I meet the right person. Definitely. I want a wife and a lot of children. I plan on being happily married and passing on the things I've learned about life to my own children. It's the most any man can do.

SHAWN:

THE **MUSIC** IS IT. IT IS WHAT BROUGHT US TOGETHER, AND IT IS WHAT KEEPS US TOGETHER.

Produced and Edited by David Cohen

Jain Lemos, Project Manager

Designed by Carrie Leeb, Leeb & Sons

Introduction and Interviews by David Sheff

Principal Photography by Nicholas Kelsh

Cover Photograph by George Holz/Onyx

Back Cover Photograph by Ron Slenzak

Additional Photographs by:
Alphonso Morris, Jr. (pages 2-3, 29, 38-39, 106), Aaron Rapoport (pages 6-7), Michael Bryant (page 93), Timothy White (page 112).

Boyz II Men express our thanks, love and praise to our Lord God and our Savior Jesus Christ.

Special Thanks also to:
The Barrett family, Jenny Barry, Carole Bidnick, Michael Bivins, Jheryl Busby, Phil Casey, George Craig, Def Jam Records, John Dukakis, Qadree El-Amin, Oscar Fields, Ken Fund, Fred Goldring, Gale Harris, Maria Hjelm, Kim Ibrahim, Sharhonda Jones, Devyani Kamdar, Michael Krassner, Johnny Lee, Daria Marmaluk-Hajioannu, Robert "Stretch" McCary, Marvin McIntyre, Sandy Miller, Alphonso Morris, Sr., Carla Morris, Dorothy, Serene and Keri Morris, Motown Records, Andy Phillips, Khalil Rountree, Thurman Sanders, Howard Schomer, Mona Scott, JoAnn Stockman, Rodney, Mark, Chris, and Tee Stockman, Tabu, OmarNetta Thomas, Jackie Thornton, Dallas Thornton, Winterland Productions

...and to all our fans all around the world! We love you all.